Die

Laughing

JOKES

For

KIDS

Die Laughing

JOKES

For

KIDS

By John Quinn

B. Street Publishing

New York, NY

For My Kids

(Who are as funny as they look.)

"Humor is just another defense against the universe." — Mel Brooks

John Quinn

Q: How do you make a tissue dance?
A: Put a little boogie in it.

The past, present, and future walked into a bar. It was tense.

A woman turns to her husband and asks, "Do you love me only because my father died and left me a fortune?"
"That's crazy. Of course not," says the husband. "I'd love you no matter who left you the money."

Q: What's the last thing a redneck says before he dies?
A: "Hey, watch this!"

A horse walks into a bar.
The bartender says, "Hey."
The horse says, "You read my
mind, buddy."

Knock, knock!
Who's there?
Gray Z.
Gray Z who?
A Gray Z mixed up kid!

Turtles think frogs are homeless.

Q: What should you do if you're
attacked by a gang of clowns?
A: Go for the juggler.

**Q: Where do pencils go for
vacation?
A: Pencil-vania.**

Knock, knock!
Who's there?
Robin.
Robin who?
Robin you! Hand over your cash!

A guy is at the supermarket doing his weekly shopping when he notices a cute new clerk running the express check-out. So when it's time to check out, he heads to her aisle and puts his groceries down on the counter: four frozen pizzas, a sports magazine and a tube of toothpaste and some mouthwash.
The clerk looks at him, smiles and says, "Single, huh?"
"Why yes," he says, "how could you tell?"
"Your breath is nasty."

Laugh at your problems, everybody else does.

A guy shows up late for work. The boss yells, "You should have been here at 8:30!"
 "Why?" asks the guy. "What happened at 8:30?"

Q: Why do bananas have to put on sunscreen before they go to the beach?
A: Because they might peel!

Knock, knock!
Who's there?
Nobel.
Nobel who?
No bell, that's why I knocked.

Officer: "Soldier, do you have change for a dollar?"
Soldier: "Sure, buddy."
Officer: "That's no way to address an officer! Let's try that again. Soldier, do you have change for a dollar?"
Soldier: "Sir, no, sir!"

Knock, knock!
Who's there?
To.
To who?
No, it's to whom?

Q: Why did the girl smear peanut butter on the road?
A: To go with the traffic jam!

Q: What jackets smell the worst?
A: Windbreakers.

A 70-year-old man is getting his annual physical. "Doc, do you think I'll live another 30 years so I can reach 100?" he asks.

"That depends," says the doctor.

"Do you smoke?"

"No."

"Do you drink?"

"No."

"Do you go on dates with women?"

"Of course not."

"Well let me ask," starts the doctor, "why the heck do you want to live another 30 years?"

A new CEO takes over at a company and decides to get rid of all the slackers. On a tour of the facilities, the CEO notices a guy leaning on a wall and can't believe the guy would just stand around.

The CEO walks up to the guy

and asks, "What are you doing here?"

"I'm just waiting to get paid," responds the man.

"How much money do you make a week?," asks the CEO.

"I make about $300 a week. Why?" says the guy.

The CEO quickly gets out his checkbook, hands the guy a check made out to cash for $1,200 and says, "Here's four weeks' pay, now get out and don't come back."

The man puts the check in his pocket and promptly walks out. Feeling pretty good about himself, the CEO looks around the room and asks, "Does anyone want to tell me what just happened here?"

From across the room a woman yells out, "Yeah, you just tipped the pizza delivery guy $1,200."

Q: Why did Adele cross the road?
A: To sing, "Hello from the other side!"

Knock, knock!
Who's there?
Aaron.
Aaron who?
Why Aaron you opening the door?

Q: Did you hear about the guys who stole a calendar?
A: They each got six months.

Knock, knock!
Who's there?
Scold
Scold who?
Scold outside, let me in!

I was wondering why the ball kept getting bigger and bigger, and then it hit me.

Two men are fishing on a riverbank when they see a funeral procession passing by. One of the men stands up, takes off his hat, and bows.
"That was a very nice thing to do," says the second man.
"Well," sniffles the first, "we were married for 25 years."

Q: What does a nosey pepper do?
A: It gets jalapeno business!

Q: Where do you find a one-legged dog?
A: Where you left him.

A man was invited to a friend's home for dinner, where he noticed that his buddy preceded every request to his wife with endearing terms, calling her honey, darling, sweetheart, pumpkin, etc. He was impressed at this, since the couple had been married more than 50 years.

While the wife was in the kitchen, he said, "I think it's wonderful that after all the years, you still call your wife those pet names."

His buddy shrugged, lowered his voice and said, "To tell you the truth, I forgot her name about 10 years ago."

Knock, knock!
Who's there?
Dishes.
Dishes who?
Dishes a nice place you got here.

Q: What did the green grape say to the purple grape?
A: "Breathe, dude!"

An old couple is sitting in church one morning, listening to a sermon, when the wife whispers, "I just let out a silent fart. What should I do?"
Her husband whispers back, "Well, for starters, you can put a new battery in your hearing aid."

Knock, knock!
Who's there?
Europe.
Europe who?
No, you're a poo.

Miss Universe pageant are fixed; every winner is from Earth.

Two wrongs don't make a right, just like parents!

A man joins a Tibetan temple. He takes a vow of silence but is allowed to say two words every year.
After 12 months of eating rice, sleeping on a wooden bed, and working 14-hour days, the man goes to the head monk and says, "More blankets."
Another year passes, and he visits the head monk and says, "More food."
The man goes through one more year eating and sleeping well, but he's isn't happy. He calls on the head monk and uses his two words to say, "I'm leaving."
"Good," the head monk replies. "You've done nothing but whine since you got here."

Q: Why couldn't the pony sing himself a lullaby?
A: He was a little hoarse.

The trouble with being punctual is that nobody's there to appreciate it.

Knock, knock!
Who's there?
Euripides.
Euripides who?
Euripides jeans and you pay for them.

Q: Why did the picture go to jail?
A: Because it was framed.

The Pope is getting into his limo one night when he turns to the limo driver and says, "You know what, before I die, I would love to drive this beautiful limo just once."

"Well," the limo driver says, "Come up here and take the wheel, Your Holiness, and I'll get in back!"

Further down the road, the limo is stopped by a policeman, who walks over to the limo, sees who's sitting in the front seat and runs back to his squad car. He calls dispatch and says, "I just pulled over someone really important and I don't know what to do."

"Well, who is it?" his dispatcher asks. "The mayor? The governor? The president?"

"I don't know exactly who he is," the officer responds, "but the Pope is his chauffeur!"

Q: What do you call a boy named Lee who no one talks to? A: Lonely.

Keep the dream alive—hit the snooze button!

Knock, knock!
Who's there?
Hanna.
Hanna who?
Hanna partridge in a pear tree!

Q: Why do they lock gas station bathrooms?
A: Because they're afraid someone will clean them.

I have all the money I'll ever need, if I die by 5:00 p.m. today.

A photon walks into a hotel. The bellhop asks, "Can I carry any of your baggage?"
The photon replies, "No thank you, I'm travelling light."

Why do Americans choose from just two people to run for president and 50 for Miss America?

Knock, knock!
Who's there?
Ya.
Ya who?
I'm excited to see you too!

Q: What do you call cheese that's not yours?
A: Nacho cheese!

Sherlock Holmes and Dr. Watson go on a camping trip, set up their tent, and fall asleep. Some hours later, Holmes wakes his faithful friend and says, "Watson, look up at the sky and tell me what you see."

Watson replies, "I see millions of stars."

"What does that tell you?"

Watson ponders for a minute. "Astronomically speaking, it tells me that there are millions of galaxies and billions of planets. Astrologically, it tells me that Saturn is in Leo. Time-wise, it appears to be approximately a quarter past 3. Meteorologically, it seems we will have a beautiful day tomorrow. What does it tell you?"

Holmes is silent a moment, then snaps, "Watson, you idiot, someone has stolen our tent."

Knock, knock!
Who's there?
Isabelle.
Isabelle who?
Isabelle working or should I
keep knocking?

The sole purpose of a child's middle name is so he can tell when he's really in trouble.

Knock, knock!
Who's there?
Irish.
Irish who?
Irish you a Merry Christmas!

The difference between in-laws and outlaws? Outlaws are wanted.

Three guys stranded on a desert island find a magic lantern containing a genie, who grants them each one wish.
The first guy wishes he was off the island and back home.
The second guy wishes the same.
The third guy says, "I'm lonely—I wish my friends were back here."

The shinbone is a device for finding furniture in a dark room.

One afternoon, a wealthy lawyer is riding in the back of his limousine when he sees two men eating grass by the roadside. He orders his driver to stop and gets out to investigate.
"Why are you eating grass?" he

asks one man.

"We don't have any money for food," the poor man replies.

"Oh, well, you can come with me to my house."

"But, sir, I have a wife and two kids with me!"

"Bring them along!" says the lawyer, before turning to the other man. "You come with us, too."

"But, Sir, I have a wife and six kids!" the man says.

"Bring them, as well!" replies the lawyer, as he heads for his limo.

They all climbed into the car. Once underway, one of the children says, "Sir, you are too kind. Thank you for taking all of us with you."

"Glad to do it, you'll love my place," says the lawyer. "The grass is almost a foot tall."

Q: Why does Humpty Dumpty look forward to winter?
A: Because he had a great fall.

Did you know that dolphins are so smart that within a few weeks of captivity they can train people to stand on the edge of the pool and throw them fish?

One day a kid says to his mom, "Hey, can I lick the bowl clean?
"No Kevin," she says. "You can flush just like the rest of us."

A guy in a restaurant asks his waiter how they prepare their chicken.
"We don't do anything special," **says the waiter. "We just tell them they're gonna die."**

A young boy at a birthday party eats too much cake and drinks too much soda and vomits all over his shirt. "Oh shoot," he says. "I threw up on my shirt. When my mom finds out she's gonna kill me."

"Not to worry," says one of the dads at the party, as he sticks a $20 bill in the boy's pocket. "Just tell her some other kid threw up on you and his mom gave you some cash to cover the cleaning bill."

The kid goes home and tells his mom the made-up story. She's suspicious and reaches into his pocket but finds two twenties. "Why are there two twenties?" she asks.

"Oh, yeah," says the boy, "the kid pooped in my pants, too."

I just lost my mood ring—not sure how I feel about that.

Knock, knock!
Who's there?
Olive.
Olive who?
Olive you!

Q: What's orange and sounds like a parrot?
A: Carrot

Knock, knock!
Who's there?
Ho-ho.
Ho-ho, who?
You know, your Santa impression could use a little work.

At the end of a job interview, the head of human resources asks the young engineer fresh out of MIT, "What starting salary were you looking for?"

The engineer decides to shoot for the moon: "I'm thinking in the range of $125,000 a year or so, depending on the benefits package."

"Hmm," says the interviewer. "Well, what would you say to five weeks' vacation, 14 paid holidays, full medical and dental, a retirement fund with company matching to 50 percent of salary, and a company car leased every two years—say, a Porsche?"

The engineer gapes and says, "Wow! Are you kidding?"

"Yeah," replies the interviewer, "but you started it."

People are making end of the world jokes like there's no tomorrow!

Knock, knock!
Who's there?
Honey bee.
Honey bee who?
Honey bee a dear and bring me some water.

Q: What's a foot long and slippery?
A: A slipper.

Q: What is the difference between a teacher and a train?
A: One says, "Spit out your gum," and the other says, "Choo, choo, choo!"

I made a belt out of wristwatches, but it turned out to be a waist of time.

Q: Why don't you ever see elephants hiding in trees?
A: Because they're really good at it.

Q: What did the big chimney say to the little chimney?
A: "You're too young to smoke."

Knock, knock!
Who's there?
Smell mop.
Smell mop who?

With great power comes great electric bills.

A guy is sitting quietly reading his paper when his wife walks up behind him and whacks him on the head with a rolled-up magazine.

"What the heck was that for?" he asks.

"That was for the piece of paper in your pants pocket with the name Mary Lou written on it," she replies.

"No, no," he pleads. "I went to the races and Mary Lou was the name of one of the horses I bet on."

"Oh honey, I'm sorry," she says. "I should have known there was a good explanation."

Three days later he was watching a ball game on TV when his wife walks up and hits him on the head again, this time with an iron skillet, which knocked him out cold. When he comes to, he asks, "What was that for?"

"Your horse just called!"

Q: Why can't you trust an atom? A: Because they make up everything.

A man goes to the doctor and says, "Doc, I broke my arm in two places."
"Well," says the doctor. "Whatever you do, don't go back to those places."

If you don't care where you are, then you ain't lost.

To err is human, to blame it on somebody else shows management potential.

Q: Why did the scarecrow get a promotion?
A: He was outstanding in his field.

A sandwich walks into a bar. The barman says: "Sorry, we don't serve food in here."

Q: "Granddad, what's the best thing about being 104?"
A: "No peer pressure."

A pig walks into a diner, orders 15 root beers, and drinks them.
The waiter asks, "Would you like to know where the bathroom is?"
"No," says the pig. "I'm the little piggy that goes wee-wee-wee all the way home."

Q: Why did the chicken go to the séance?
A: To get to the other side.

A duck walks into a drugstore and puts a tube of lipstick on the counter.
The cashier says, "That'll be $2.49."
The duck saus, "Put it on my bill."

Q: What has more lives than a cat?
A: A frog; it croaks every night.

After a talking sheepdog gets all the sheep in the pen, he reports back to the farmer. "All 40 accounted for," says the sheepdog.
"But I only have 36 sheep," says the farmer.
"I know, but I rounded them up."

A hiker gets lost in the woods and spends the next three days wandering around with no food. Finally, he spots a bald eagle on a ledge, hits it with a big rock, and begins eating it raw.

A park ranger stumbles on the scene and arrests the hiker for killing an endangered species.

In court the hiker explains that he was on the edge of starvation and had no choice.

"Considering the circumstances, I find you not guilty," says the judge. "But I have to ask—what did the eagle taste like?"

"Well, your honor," the hiker says, "if I had to describe it, I'd say it tasted something like a cross between a whooping crane and a spotted owl."

A man goes to a psychiatrist and says, "Doc, my brother's crazy, he thinks he's a chicken."
The doctor says, "Why don't you have him committed?"
"We would," says the guy, "but we need the eggs."

Q: Why is gambling outlawed in Africa?
A: Too many cheetahs!

Q: Have you heard about the new restaurant called Karma?
A: There's no menu, you just get what you deserve.

Q: What nails do carpenters hate to hit?
A: Fingernails.

Three elderly sisters are living together in a big old house.

The first sister decides to take a bath. She goes upstairs, turns on the bath water, disrobes, and is about to dip her toe into the water when she stops and yells, "Sister, oh, sister! I forget! Am I getting in or getting out?"

The second sister says, "Just a minute, sister...I'll be right up!" Half way up the stairs she stops...turns around and yells, "Sister? I forget! Am I coming or going?"

The third sister shakes her head and says to herself, "Thank you, God. At least I'm not as bad as either of them, knock on wood." And she knocks three times on her head. She then yells out, "Just a minute, sisters, someone's at the door!"

A young boy enters a barbershop and the barber whispers to his customer, "This is the dumbest kid in the world. Watch while I prove it to you."

The barber puts a dollar bill in one hand and two quarters in the other, then calls the boy over and asks, "Which do you want, son?"

The boy takes the quarters and leaves.

"What did I tell you?" says the barber. "That kid never learns!"

Later, when the customer leaves, he sees the same young boy coming out of the ice cream store and says, "Hey, son—may I ask you a question? Why did you take the quarters instead of the dollar bill?"

The boy licked his cone and replies, "Because the day I take the dollar, the game is over!"

It's Game 7 of the Stanley Cup Final and a man makes his way to his seat right at center ice. He sits down, noticing that the seat next to him is empty. He leans over and asks his neighbor if someone will be sitting there.

"No" says the neighbor. "The seat is empty."

"That's incredible," says the man. "Who would have a seat like this for the Stanley Cup and not use it?"

"Well, actually, the seat belongs to me," says the man. "I was supposed to come with my wife, but she passed away. This is the first Stanley Cup we haven't been to together since we got married."

"Oh, I'm so sorry to hear that. That's terrible. But couldn't you find someone else, a friend or relative to take the seat?"

"Afraid not," he says. "They're all at the funeral."

Knock, knock!
Who's there?
Lettuce.
Lettuce who?
Lettuce in and you'll find out.

Two campers are hiking in the woods when one is bitten on his butt by a rattlesnake.

"I'll go into town for a doctor," the other says. He runs ten miles to a small town and finds the town's only doctor, who is delivering a baby.

"I can't leave," the doctor says. "But here's what to do. Take a knife, cut a little X where the bite is, suck out the poison and spit it out." The guy runs back to his friend, who's in terrible agony.

"What did the doctor say?" his friend asks.

"He says you're gonna die."

Three kids are sitting around the breakfast table. The mother asks the oldest boy what he'd like to eat.

"I'll have some damn French toast," he says. The mother is outraged at his language, hits him, and sends him upstairs. She asks the middle child what he wants.

"Well, I guess that leaves more damn French toast for me," he says.

The mother smacks him and sends him upstairs as well. Finally she asks the youngest son what he wants for breakfast.

"I don't know," he says meekly, "but I definitely don't want any damn French toast."

Preventing childhood obesity is as easy as taking candy from a baby.

I remember the last thing my grandpa said to me before he kicked the bucket. He said, "Hey, how far do you think I can kick this bucket?"

A guy goes to the doctor and after getting a thorough exam the doctor returns looking grim.

"I'm sorry to tell you this," says the doctor, "but you suffer from a terminal illness and have only 10 to live."

"What do you mean, 10?" yells the guy. "Ten what? Months? Weeks?"

"Nine..."

Q: What is the difference between a snowman and a snowwoman?
A: Snowballs.

Little Patrick comes home from school and sits down at the kitchen table.

"How was school today, Patrick?" asks his mother.

"It was really great mom," says Patrick. "Today we made explosives!"

"Oh, wow," says his mom. "They do very fancy stuff with you these days. What will you do at school tomorrow?"

"What school?"

The reason grandchildren and grandparents get along so well is because they have a common enemy.

If you keep your feet firmly on the ground, you'll have trouble putting your pants on.

A police officer pulls a car over for speeding and goes up to the guy and says, "Can you identify yourself, sir?"
The guy pulls out his mirror and says, "Yes, it's me."

After an examination, a doctor says to his patient "I have bad news and really bad news."
"Oh no, " says the man. "What's the really bad news?"
"You have cancer."
"Yikes," says the man. "Well, what's the bad news?"
"You also have Alzheimer's."
"Oh, well," says the man. "At least I don't have cancer."

If you can't be positive, just be double negative.

Q: What did the right eye say to the left eye?
A: Between you and me, something smells.

A guy finds a sheep wandering in his neighborhood and takes it to the police station. The desk sergeant tells the guy to just take the sheep to the zoo.
The next day, the sergeant spots the same guy walking down the street with the sheep.
"I thought I told you to take that sheep to the zoo," says the sergeant.
"I know, I did," the guy responds. "Today I'm taking him to the movies."

Change is inevitable, except from a vending machine.

A teacher asks her students to use the word "beans" in a sentence. "My father grows beans," says one girl.
"My mother cooks beans," says a boy.
A third student stands up and says, "We are all human beans."

I intend to live forever. So far, so good.

Q: How many snowboarders does it take to screw in a light bulb?
A: 50: 3 to die trying, 1 to actually pull it off, and 46 others to say, "Man, I could do that!"

Whoever invented knock-knock jokes should get a no bell prize.

A husband and wife are driving through Illinois. As they approach the town of Cairo, they start debating its pronunciation. They finally arrive and find someplace to have lunch. At the counter, the husband asks the woman, "Can you please settle an argument for us? How do you pronounce where we are?"
"No problem," says the woman. "It's Bur-ger Kiiing."

Q: Did you hear about the kidnapping at school?
A: It's okay. He woke up.

Q: What did one toilet say to the other?
A: You look a bit flushed.

When 80-year-old Robert went for his annual check-up, the doctor asked if he had any complaints. "My only problem is that I sometimes have to get up in the middle of the night to go to the bathroom," Robert says. "But I'm blessed. God knows my eyesight is bad so he turns the light on when I pee, and he turns it off when I'm done!"

Later that day, the doctor called Robert's wife: "Your husband's test results were fine, but he said something strange that has been bugging me. He claims that God turns the light on and off for him when he uses the bathroom at night."

"That old fool!" Betsy exclaims. "He's been peeing in the refrigerator again!"

Q: What's the difference between a 16" pizza and a jazz musician?
A: A 16" pizza can feed a family of four.

Q: Why are mountains not just funny?
A: Because they're also hill areas.

A bargain is something you don't need at a price you can't resist.

Q: What do computers snack on?
A: Microchips!

A man got hit in the head with a can of Coke. Yeah, he's all right because it was a soft drink.

A young boy asks his father, "Where do babies come from?" "Adam and Eve made babies," says the father. "Then their babies became adults and made babies, and so on."
The boy then goes to his mother and asks her the same question. "We started out as monkeys," explains the mom. "Then we evolved to become like we are now."
The boy runs back to his father and says, "You lied to me. Mommy says we came from monkeys."
"Oh no," says the father. "Your mom is talking about her side of the family."

Q: What do you call a pig that does karate?
A: A pork chop.

An elderly couple notice that they're getting a lot more forgetful, so they decide to go to the doctor, who tells them that they should start writing things down to help them remember. They go home and the woman tells her husband to get her a bowl of ice cream.

"You might want to write it down," she says.

"No, I can remember that you want a bowl of ice cream," he says.

"And put whipped cream on it. Write that down!"

"I can remember some whipped cream!"

"Put a cherry on top. Write that down, too."

"No, I got it. You want a bowl of ice cream with whipped cream and a cherry on top."

The husband goes to the kitchen to get the ice cream but doesn't come back for a long time. Finally he comes out to his wife and hands her a plate of eggs and bacon. She stares at the plate for a moment, then looks at her husband and yells, "You forgot the toast!"

If you ever get cold, just stand in the corner of a room for a while. They're normally around 90 degrees.

A man is at the doctor's office for a check-up when the doctor walks in. "I have good news and bad news," says the doctor. "The good news is you have 24 hours left to live." "Oh my god!" screams the man. "What's the bad news?" "The bad news is I should have told you this yesterday."

Fountain of Youth jokes never get old.

An English captain is walking his ship when a sailor rushes to him and says, "An enemy ship is approaching!"

"Stay calm," says the captain. "And go get my red shirt."

"Of course, captain," says the sailor. "But do you mind if I ask why?"

"If I get injured, I don't want you men to see me bleed and lose hope."

Just then, another sailor runs up and says, "Sir, twenty more enemy ships are approaching!"

The captain thinks for a moment and then says, "You better bring me my brown pants, too."

Q: Why did the school kids eat their homework?
A: Because their teacher told them it was a piece of cake.

A man calls his child's doctor and says, "My son just snatched my pen when I was writing and swallowed it. What should I do?"
"Until I can come over," says the doctor, "write with another pen."

Q: Why did the fish blush?
A: Because it saw the ocean's bottom.

Q: How did the buffalo say goodbye to his kid?
A: Bison.

At a cocktail party, one woman says to another, "Aren't you wearing your wedding ring on the wrong finger?"
"Yes," the other woman replies. "I married the wrong man."

Knock, knock!
Who's there?
Broken pencil.
Broken pencil who?
Oh, forget it. This joke is pointless.

A man in a movie theater notices what looks like a fly eating popcorn sitting next to him.
"Are you a fly?" asks the man, surprised.
"Yes," the fly responds.
"What are you doing at the movies?"
"Well, I liked the book."

A burglar breaks into a house one night. He picks up a CD player to place in his bag and a strange voice echoes from the dark, saying, "Jesus is watching you."
He nearly jumps out of his skin, clicks his flashlight off, and freezes. After a few minutes, his shakes his head, clicks the light on, and begins searching for more valuables. Just as he pulls the stereo out so he can disconnect the wires, he hears, "Jesus is watching you."
He shines his light around frantically, looking for the source of the voice. Finally, in the corner of the room, he sees a parrot.
"Did you say that?" he hisses at the parrot.
"Yep," the parrot confesses. "I'm just trying to warn you."
"Warn me, huh? Who in the world are you?"
"Moses," replies the bird.

"Moses?" the burglar laughs. "What kind of people would name a bird Moses?"
"The same kind of people who would name a Rottweiler Jesus."

Did you hear about the guy whose whole left side was cut off? He's all right now.

Two flies sitting on a dog poo. One farts. The other says, "Do you mind? I'm eating my dinner!"

Knock, knock!
Who's there?
Little old lady.
Little old lady who?
Wow, I didn't know you could yodel!

Q: Why are redneck murder cases toughest to solve?
A: There are no dental records.

Two fortune tellers meet on the street. The first says, "You're fine. How am I?"

A big buck just took off with my car. I guess you could say it was common-deered.

Q: What's blue and smells like red paint?
A: Blue paint.

It was love at first sight. Then I took a second look!

A man dies and goes up to the Pearly Gates to stand before Saint Peter. Peter tells him, "Before you meet with God, I should tell you — we've looked over your life, and to be honest you really didn't do anything particularly good or bad. We're not really sure what to do with you. Can you tell us anything you did that can help us make a decision?"

The newly arrived soul thinks for a moment and replies, "Well, yeah, once I was driving along and came upon a man who was being harassed by a group of thugs. So I pulled over, got my baseball bat out from behind my seat and went up to the leader of the thugs. He was a big, muscular guy with a ring pierced through his lip. Well, I tore the ring out of his lip, and told him

that his gang had better stop bothering this guy or they would have to deal with me!"
"Wow that's impressive," says Peter. "When did this happen?"
"About three minutes ago."

Knock, knock!
Who's there?
Nana.
Nana who?
Nana your business, that's who!

When my friend told me to stop impersonating flamingos, I had to put my foot down.

Two antennas met on a roof, fell in love and got married. The ceremony wasn't much, but the reception was excellent.

After robbing a bank, a blonde, a brunette and a redhead duck into an alley where they hide in potato sacks. The cops first go to the sack with the brunette in it and kick it. The brunette says, "Meow, meow!" They go to the sack with the redhead in it and kick it. The redhead says, "Woof, woof." Last, they kick the sack with the blonde in it and she says, "Po-ta-to, po-ta-to!"

A guy is walking past an insane asylum when he hears the residents inside chanting, "Thirteen! Thirteen! Thirteen!" Curious, he finds a hole in the wall and looks in. Immediately, he's poked in the eye. A second later everyone inside starts chanting, "Fourteen! Fourteen! Fourteen!"

Q: What did the little fish say when he swam into a wall?
A: Dam!

Yo' mama's so dump, she walked into an antique shop and asked, "What's new?"

Two guys are walking down a dark street when a mugger approaches them with a gun and demands their money. They both grudgingly pull out their wallets and begin taking out their cash. Just then, one guy turns to the other, hands him his cash, and says, "Hey, here's that hundred bucks I owe you."

If 4 out of 5 people suffer from diarrhea, does that mean that one enjoys it?

Q: If you have 13 apples in one hand and 10 oranges in the other, what do you have?
A: Big hands.

A blonde is watching the news with her husband when the newscaster announces that six Brazilian men died in a skydiving accident, and she starts sobbing uncontrollably. "It's sad, but they were skydiving," says her husband. "They knew the risk involved." "I know," says the blonde. "But how many is a Brazillian?"

Knock, knock!
Who's there?
Mikey.
Mikey who?
Mikey doesn't fit in the keyhole.

A man thinks he's a dog so he goes to see a psychiatrist.
"It's terrible, doc," the man says. "I walk around on all fours, I keep barking in the middle of the night and I can't go beyond our yard anymore."
"Okay," says the psychiatrist. "Have a seat on the couch"
"Oh, no," says the man. "I'm not allowed on the couch."

Two men are hiking in a forest when they see a bear. One man quickly starts changing into a pair of running shoes. The other guy looks at him and says, "That's stupid. You can't outrun a bear."
"I know," says the first guy. "But I can outrun you."

Q: Why don't blind people skydive?
A: Scares the heck out of the dog.

A cruise ship passes a small desert island. Everyone is watching as a ratty-looking bearded man runs out on the beach and starts shouting and waving his hands.
"Who's that?" asks one of the passengers.
"I don't know," replies the captain. "But every year we sail past and he goes nuts."

Two muffins go into an oven. One muffin turns to the other and says, "Wow it's hot in here." "Holy cow," the other muffin says. "A talking muffin!"

A bus is a vehicle that runs twice as fast when you are after it as when you are in it.

Q: What's the best thing about Switzerland?
A: I don't know, but the flag is a big plus.

Two drivers climb out of their cars after colliding at an intersection. One pulls a flask from his pocket and says, "Here, have a slug of whiskey to calm your nerves." "Thanks," says the other guy, talking a swig. "Here you go." "No thanks," says the man. "The cops will be here soon."

If the No. 2 pencil is the most popular, why is it still No. 2?

After dinner, two elderly women retire to the kitchen and leave their husbands to chat. One of the men says, "Last night we went out to a great new restaurant."

"What's it called?" asks the other man.

The first man thinks for a second and finally says, "Ah, what's the name of that red flower you give someone you love?"

"A carnation?" asks his friend.

"No, no. The other one."

"A poppy?"

"No!" growls the man. "The one with the thorns."

"Oh, you mean a rose."

"Yes, that's it," the first husband says. He then turns toward the kitchen and yells, "Rose, what is the name of that restaurant we went to last night?"

Knock, knock!
Who's there?
Cash.
Cash who?
I didn't realize you were some
kind of nut!

Q: How do wives start a normal
conversation?
A: Hey, are you even listening?

I'd tell you the joke about the
robotic mining machine that
started attacking humans, but
it'll probably bore you to death.

Two snowmen are standing in a
field. One says to the other,
"Funny, I smell carrots, too."

A man is driving down the street, sweating because he has an important meeting and can't find parking. Looking up toward heaven, the man says, "Lord, take pity on me. If you find me a parking space, I'll go to church every Sunday for the rest of my life and give up gambling and never swear again."
Just then, a parking space appears.
The man looks up and says, "Never mind, I just found one."

Do not argue with an idiot. He will drag you down to his level and beat you with experience.

Q: What do you call a nun on a motorcycle?
A: Virgin mobile.

Q: What's the difference between a guitar and a fish?
A: You can tune a guitar, but you can't tuna fish.

A woman's husband has been slipping in and out of a coma for several weeks. One day, he motions for her to come nearer. As she sits by him, he whispers, "You know what? You have been with me all through the bad times. When I got fired, you were there to support me. When my business failed, you were there. When my health started failing you were still by my side. You know what?"
"What my dear," she asked, her eyes full of tears.
"I think you're bad luck—get the heck away from me!"

Every time you ingest food coloring, you dye a little inside.

I threw a boomerang once and now I live in perpetual fear. If security is posted at the Samsung store, does that make them Guardians of the Galaxy?

A woman gets on a bus with her baby and the bus driver says, "Wow, that's the ugliest baby I've ever seen!"
The woman walks to the rear of the bus and sits down, fuming.
"What's wrong," asks a man sitting next to her.
"The bus driver just insulted me," answers the woman.
"You should go back up there and tell him off," says the man. "Go on, I'll hold your poodle for you."

Q: What's Beethoven's favorite fruit?
A: Ba-na-na-naaa!

I asked God for a bike, but I know God doesn't work that way. So I stole a bike and asked for forgiveness.

Knock, knock!
Who's there?
Luke.
Luke who?
Luke through the keyhole and you'll see!

Whoever coined the phrase "quiet as a mouse" has never stepped on one.

People who are gluten free get a lot of grief, but I give them credit for going against the grain.

A three-legged dog walks into a saloon in the Old West. He slides up to the bar and announces: "I'm looking for the man who shot my paw."

Knock, knock!
Who's there?
Atch.
Atch who?
Bless you!

I want to die peacefully in my sleep, like my grandfather. Not screaming and yelling like the passengers in his car.

Q: What did zero say to eight?
A: Nice belt.

Knowledge is knowing a tomato is a fruit; wisdom is not putting it in a fruit salad.

I have sensitive teeth and I'm afraid I'll say something that will hurt their fillings.

Knock, knock!
Who's there?
Tank.
Tank who?
You're welcome!

You know, it's bad luck to be superstitious.

A woman has twins and decides to give them up for adoption. One of them is sent to a family in Egypt and is named "Amal." The other goes to a family in Spain, where the family names him "Juan."

Years later, Juan tracks down his biological mother and sends a picture of himself. Upon receiving the picture, the mom tells her husband that she wished she also had a picture of Amal.

"But they are twins," says the husband. "If you've seen Juan, you've seen Amal."

Laugh and the world laughs with you. Snore and you sleep alone.

John Quinn

RIDDLES

Q: What's a seven letter word containing thousands of letters?
A: A mailbox.

Q: When you need me you throw me away. When you don't need me you bring me back. What am I?
A: A trash bag.

Q: Poor people have it. Rich people need it. If you eat it you die. What is it?
A: Nothing.

Q: What comes down but never goes up?
A: Rain.

Q: I'm tall when I'm young and I'm short when I'm old. What am I?
A: A candle.

Q: Mary's father has 5 daughters – Nana, Nene, Nini, Nono. What is the fifth daughter's name?
A: If you answered Nunu, you are wrong. It's Mary.

Q: How can a pants pocket be empty and still have something in it?
A: It can have a hole in it.

Q: What is the longest word in the dictionary?
A: Smiles, because there is a mile between each "s."

Q: In a one-story pink house, there was a pink person, a pink cat, a pink fish, a pink computer, a pink chair, a pink table, a pink telephone, a pink shower– everything was pink! What color were the stairs?
A: There weren't any stairs. It was a one-story house.

Q: Throw away the outside and cook the inside, then eat the outside and throw away the inside. What is it?
A: Corn on the cob.

Q: A man is driving his truck. His lights are not on. The moon is not out. Up ahead, a woman is crossing the street. How can he see her?
A: It's daytime.

Q: What word becomes shorter when you add two letters to it?
A: Short.

Q: What can you catch but not throw?
A: A cold.

Q: What is at the end of a rainbow?
A: The letter "w."

Q: What travels around the world but stays in one spot?
A: A stamp.

Q: How do you organize a space party?
A: You planet.

Q: What occurs once in a minute, twice in a moment and never in one thousand years?
A: The letter "m."

Q: What has four eyes but can't see?
A: Mississippi.

Q: We see it once in a year, twice in a week, and never in a day. What is it?
A: The letter "e."

Q: You walk into a room with a match, a kerosene lamp, a candle, and a fireplace. Which do you light first?
A: The match.

Q: A man leaves home and turns left three times, only to return home facing two men wearing masks. Who are those two men?
A: A catcher and an umpire.

Q: Which weighs more, a pound of feathers or a pound of bricks?
A: Neither, they both weigh one pound.

Q: If a blue house is made out of blue bricks, a yellow house is made out of yellow bricks and a pink house is made out of pink bricks, what is a green house made of?
A: Glass.

Q: How many months have 28 days?
A: All 12 months.

Q: If I have it, I don't share it. If I share it, I don't have it. What is it?
A: A secret.

**Q: How do you make the number one disappear?
A: Add the letter "g" and it's gone.**

Q: Who makes it, but has no need of it. Who buys it, but has no use for it. Who uses it but can neither see nor feel it. What is it?
A: A coffin.

**Q: What starts with "e," ends with "e," and has only one letter in it?
A: An envelope.**

Q: What has one head, one foot and four legs?
A: A bed.

Q: If you were in a race and passed the person in 2nd place, what place would you be in?
A: 2nd place.

Q: How many letters are in The Alphabet?
A: There are 11 letters in The Alphabet.

Q: How can you spell cold with two letters?
A: IC (icy).

Q: John's father had three sons: Snap, Crackle, and…?
A: John.

Q: What has a head, a tail, is brown and has no legs?
A: A penny.

Q: What gets bigger and bigger as you take more away from it?
A: A hole.

Q: How many books can you put into an empty backpack?
A: One; after that it's not empty.

Q: What breaks when you say it?
A: Silence.

Q: How far can a fox run into the woods?
A: Only halfway—then he's running out of it.

Q: What kind of coat is always wet when you put it on?
A: A coat of paint.

Q: What has hands but cannot clap?
A: A clock.

Q: What starts with the letter "t," is filled with "t" and ends in "t"?
A: A teapot.

Q: How many seconds are there in one year?
A: 12 of them: January 2nd, February 2nd, March 2nd...

Q: What has 13 hearts, but no other organs?
A: A deck of playing cards.

Q: What do you call a bear without an ear?
A: A "b."

Q: What do you break before you use it?
A: An egg.

Q: What is the tallest building in the entire world?
A: The library, because it has so many stories.

Q: Why is the letter "a" like a flower?
A: Because the "b" is always after it.

Q: Which is the most curious letter?
A: "Y?"

Q: A man rode in to town on Friday, and left two days later on Friday. How can that be?
A: His horse is named Friday.

Q: What do zebras have that no other animals have?
A: Baby zebras.

Q: Why can't someone living in Maine be buried in New Jersey?
A: Because they're still living.

Q: Which month has 28 days?
A: All of them.

Q: What is easy to get into, but hard to get out of?
A: Trouble.

Stay out of trouble kids, and never loose your sense of humor!

Made in the USA
San Bernardino, CA
15 December 2019